EILEEN AGAR

This book is from a series about Modern Women Artists published by Eiderdown Books.

Other titles available from the same series:

To order books, please visit eiderdownbooks.com

EILEEN AGAR

Laura Smith

EIDERDOWN
BOOKS

MODERN WOMEN ARTISTS

1. *Ceremonial Hat for Eating Bouillabaisse*, 1936, photograph

I have spent my life in revolt against convention, trying to bring colour and light and a sense of the mysterious to daily existence. [. . .] one must have a hunger for new colour, new shapes and new possibilities of discovery.[1]

Eileen Agar (1899–1991) was one of the most adventurous and prolific artists of her generation. Throughout her 80-year career she synthesised elements of two of the twentieth century's most significant artistic tendencies – Cubism and Surrealism – in a diverse practice that moved freely through painting, photography, collage and sculpture. Fascinated by classical art, ancient mythologies, the natural world, sexual pleasure and her own biography, Agar mined these subjects for the forms and content that filled her works. Despite reservations about being called a Surrealist, Agar was one of the only British women included in the International Surrealist Exhibition (1936), she was a member of the London Group[2] from 1934 and held several major retrospective exhibitions during her lifetime. In 1988 she published an autobiography, *A Look at My Life*, and was elected to the Royal Academy in 1990.

Agar was excited by the Surrealists' desire to paint the subconscious but suspicious about the idea of wholly working from dreams. For her, Surrealism provided 'the interpenetrating of reason and unreason,'[3] and she used it to inject wit, irreverence and corporeality into the more analytical realms of Cubism and abstraction. In doing so, Agar created a distinct and spirited style that significantly impacted twentieth-century culture.

1

The Villa of Lilacs to Fitzroy Square: from Buenos Aires to London

Eileen Agar was born in Buenos Aires on 1 December 1899. Her father was a Scottish industrialist and her mother was an American heiress. They were wealthy and privileged, if a little eccentric. Agar described her childhood home Quinta la Lila (The Villa of Lilacs) as full of balloons, hoops and St Bernard dogs. She remembered big exotic gardens, picking peaches in the summer, and a pony she named 'Strawberry Cream'. Wind features prominently in her recollections of Argentina, as do the swarming plagues of locusts that would visit in the autumn. In the winter, she and her two sisters would be made to wear furs, not for warmth as it was rarely cold enough, but as a way of demonstrating the Agars' wealth. Likewise, when the family travelled to Britain, which they did every two years, her mother apparently insisted on bringing a cow for fresh milk and an orchestra so that they would be surrounded by music.

Despite these flamboyant, and one might say, surreal beginnings, both Agar's mother and nanny were strict disciplinarians and Agar was a rebellious child. Her burgeoning interest in art frustrated her mother. Agar would spend hours drawing and reading rather than practising her needlework or comportment. So, aged six she was sent to boarding school in Dorset, England. In 1911, when her father retired and the rest of her family relocated to Britain, she attended Heathfield School in Ascot. Here pupils were encouraged to each keep a small pet and while most girls chose a rabbit or hamster, Agar opted for a grass snake. Perhaps her most significant experience at Heathfield though, were her lessons with the painter Lucy Kemp-Welch RA, who encouraged Agar to 'always have something to do with art.'[4]

Unbeknownst to her parents, Agar's education was being built on strong artistic foundations, which, combined with the trauma of the First World War, led her to pursue a more unconventional life: 'the war had left a scar ... I wanted to do something that I considered more worthwhile than the usual repetitive routine of marrying and having a brood of children.'[5] A rift began to grow between Agar and her parents, who admonished the idea of a career in art. However, in 1920 Lady George Clerk – friend to artists Renoir, Bonnard and Monet – visited the Agar home and, after seeing Agar's drawings, implored her to interview at the Slade School of Fine Art. Because of Lady Clerk's backing, her parents consented and Agar interviewed with Henry Tonks (Slade Professor of Fine Art) the same year. Tonks was encouraging but told her to return when she was older, and in the meantime to attend Brook Green School of Art in Hammersmith. Here, under the guidance of artist and teacher Leon Underwood, Agar learnt 'the ABC of art'[6] and the following year took up her place at the Slade.

Tonks' approach to teaching was quite authoritarian and though she valued her time at the Slade, Agar found it restrictive. Her relationship with her parents deteriorated and she felt increasingly trapped. In 1924 she left the family home, ran away to Cornwall and shaved her head 'to celebrate my new freedom!'[7] She then travelled to Paris and Spain with fellow Slade student Robin Bartlett, who she married in 1925, to her parents' disapproval (he was working-class). The same year, Agar destroyed the majority of her work, unfulfilled and dissatisfied with its development. Her father died soon after and, though critical of her life-choices, he left her a small inheritance that would sustain her for many years. Then, in 1926, Agar met the Hungarian writer, Joseph Bard. She described the encounter as 'the shock effect of a putting out of place, creating the sharpness of a new focus.'[8] Where Bartlett had been 'the escape hatch that freed me from the clutches of my family',[9] Agar's relationship with Bard was a more intense and generative one. In 1927 she left Bartlett to begin a new life with Bard in London, taking a flat in Fitzroy Square in a building that had previously been home to Virginia Woolf.

Finding Her Voice: Early Abstractions and International Adventures

In Fitzroy Square, Agar was able to paint with the self-assurance that she had previously lacked when: 'everything I had done was academic and timid in approach, careful of other men's teaching … Now, without thinking, I was free of all constraint and painted as naturally as I walked or talked.'[10] She began to question the limitations of the education she had received and was discontented with imitating the old masters: 'it disturbed me to see youthful girls standing in front of Masaccio or something and trying to copy it.'[11] She made the decision to embark on a self-portrait, representative of her new found confidence. *Self-portrait* (1927, Fig. 2) is the result, painted in thick impasto straight onto the canvas; it has a fresh, sunlit look with each form differentiated from the other through variations in texture and colour, and the green of her top reflected in the shadows on her face. As a self-portrait, it expresses both Agar's approach to expression and her self-reliance as a worthy painter: 'I certainly felt more positive in my approach than I had at the Slade under Tonks; for I had thrown off the shackles and started a new life, and I painted what may be considered my first successful work.'[12]

From 1927–8 Agar and Bard lived between London and Portofino, Italy where they met and befriended the poet Ezra Pound. In 1929, keen to learn more about European painting, Agar (and Bard) moved to Paris, where they met the Surrealists André Breton and Paul Éluard. In Paris, Agar also began painting lessons with the Czech Cubist, František Foltýn who taught her 'about sensitivity to form while trying to cultivate colour, planes and composition.'[13] Agar was beginning to think about non-figurative painting and enjoying her investigations through abstraction. However, she was also drawn to the sensuality and irrationality of Surrealism, which, for her, offered

2. *Self-portrait*, 1927, oil on canvas

an important counterbalance to the idealism and harmony of pure abstraction: she saw Surrealism as capable of re-humanising the impersonal rationality of Cubism. These early explorations – taken in tandem – into Cubism and Surrealism, allowed Agar to synthesise elements from both of these important artistic tendencies and cultivate a unique style that would endure for the rest of her creative life.

One of the first works she made in her new experimental style, *Flying Pillar* (1928–30, Fig. 3) (later renamed *Three Symbols*) was Agar's 'first attempt at an imaginative approach to painting and although the result was surreal, it was not done with that intention'.[14] Through a floating composition, the painting denotes the meeting of the classical world with the modern, with structures from three cultures: a Greek column to represent the ancient world, a Gothic cathedral (Notre Dame) as a symbol of Medieval Christianity, and a bridge by Gustave Eiffel to symbolise the advent of modernity. *Flying Pillar* was begun in Paris and completed in Kensington, London, when she and Bard returned to England in 1930. Here, Agar painted her most Cubist work – and the only one to survive unaltered – *Movement in Space* (1931, Fig. 4). Foltýn's teachings are evident in this work, in the muted colour tones and flattened composition, though Agar's budding interest in organic shapes and embryonic forms is also clear.

> 'I had begun to free myself from the cul-de-sac of representational painting by learning the principles of abstract painting, and experimenting with content as well as form.'[15]

Agar and Bard commissioned Agar's friend from Brook Green, the architect Rodney Thomas, to design the living space and studios in their Kensington flat, where Agar created a huge, ever-changing collage of images, drawings, postcards and photographs.[16] Almost an artwork in its own right, this studio became

3. *Three Symbols (Flying Pillar)*, 1928–30, oil on canvas

an enduring source of inspiration. Objects changed constantly – textures, fabrics, sculpted heads, stone and metal shapes: 'throughout the 1930s my studio transformed itself, one day suggesting Magritte, the next de Chirico … I was collecting and storing all the time, surrounding myself with the raw material which would be transmuted into paintings and objects. In fact, the flat must have changed like a sea-wreck cast up by the tide.'[17] In this highly stimulating environment, the couple founded and published four issues of a new journal: *The Island*. Edited by Bard and Leon Underwood, it was 'intended to be a quarterly magazine dedicated to the plastic arts, poetry and the imagination.'[18] Agar contributed writing, woodcuts and ideas to all four issues which included texts, poetry and artworks by other creatives in their circle, including Gertrude Hermes, Catherine Carswell, Naomi Mitchinson, Henry Moore, Ezra Pound, and even Gandhi. In the first issue Agar included a small engraving titled *The Bird. Two Lovers* (1931, Fig. 5), a semi-abstract composition that can be read as a bird or as two figures intertwined. Technically, Agar drew on the engraving expertise at Underwood's school. Using scratching techniques to emphasise and gradate between light and dark she played on the tension between flatness and decorative line, resulting in a taut fusion of abstract composition and symbolic subject matter.

Agar was becoming aware of her identity as a woman artist and developing a clear idea of the impact that her gender was having on her career. Through her writings and engravings for *The Island,* she was building a theory that she called 'womb magic': 'in Europe, the importance of the unconscious in all forms of Literature and Art establishes the dominance of a feminine order over the classical and more masculine order. Apart from rampant and hysterical militarism, there is no male element left in Europe, for the intellectual and rational

4. (above) *Movement in Space*, 1931, oil on canvas
5. (below) *The Bird. Two Lovers*, 1931, woodcut

conception of life has given way to a more miraculous creative interpretation, and artistic and imaginative life is under the sway of womb-magic.'[19] This thinking informed most of her work during the early 1930s. *Family Trio* (Fig. 6) – an engraving (1931), watercolour (1931) and oil painting (1934) – echoes these ideas, wherein three figures recur: one representing ancient patriarchy; another central, floating feminine form straddles land and sea; while an embryonic, emergent child forms in the sea, under a crescent moon. Here the natural, animal and human kingdoms coalesce toward a universal organicism, twilight in colour and budding with nascent hope.

The Autobiography of an Embryo (1933–4, Fig. 7) is perhaps the most demonstrative of Agar's theory of 'womb magic' and is often described as an early masterpiece. A huge, four-section, horizontal painting that depicts an eternal cycle of renewal and evolution: 'I was looking at all sorts of drawings of early venuses and early work ... because I thought that would give me an idea of how humankind gradually evolved.'[20] The work has a complex, rhythmic energy that repeats and echoes across the four planes. Classical influences are evident in Agar's abstract shapes and patterns, which resemble draped figures, antique statues and Etruscan symbols. Shells, wings, plant-like structures, fossils, cells and embryonic forms, alongside African masks and Italian Renaissance portraiture are also combined with modern elements, such as a brick wall or graffiti-like-heads, like a finely tuned collage. Instead of the seven ages of man, Agar gives us the four ages of a foetus. She saw this painting in universal terms, describing it as 'a celebration of life, not only a single one, but Life in general on this particular and moving planet.'[21] The painting is intended to be read from left to right, like a storyboard, and her use of familiar imagery was a deliberate device: 'I wanted to make it into a story as if told to a child, not into a scientific thesis'.[22] *The Autobiography of an Embryo* is complex but certainly not chaotic, and though dense, its composition is harmoniously and intuitively layered and balanced.

6. *Family Trio*, 1931, watercolour

7. *The Autobiography of an Embryo*, 1933–4, oil on board

Sea Monsters, Shells and Stones:
Assemblage, Collage and Surrealist Beginnings

Of course, collage was a central and vital component to Agar's artistic practice. Invented by the Cubists and used extensively by the Surrealists, it is no surprise that for Agar it became a treasured medium. One that she described as: 'a displacement of the banal by the fertile intervention of chance or coincidence'.[23] In 1935, Agar and Bard took a house for the summer at Swanage, Dorset. One evening the couple were invited to a dinner with Paul and Margaret Nash. Nash, who was in Dorset compiling *The Dorset Shell Guide* for Shell-Mex, was an artist Agar had long-admired and apparently, he felt the same about her. So began an artistic understanding that became an emotional attachment, and an intense and productive friendship that endured until Nash's death in 1946. Together, Agar and Nash discovered 'the strange poetic atmosphere . . . in Swanage: the two Greek columns (recalling de Chirico?) standing for no apparent reason on the drive of the Grosvenor Hotel, the lonely swan buffeted by the waves, and countless other details.'[24] Swanage became an important site of inspiration for both artists: and it was there that, whilst walking with Bard on the beach, Agar came across a curious item in the sand – a long snaky monster with a bird's beak, covered in stones, shells and marine deposits. It turned out to be an old anchor chain, metamorphosised by the sea. Knowing that the monster would be exciting to Nash, Agar fetched him and together they painted and photographed it extensively. It features in Nash's well-known work *Swanage* (c.1936)[25] and a number of collages and watercolours (now lost) by Agar. Agar also brought the monster home to London, hoping to use it in an assemblage but sadly it was destroyed during the war.

Trawling for objects became a favourite working method for Agar, and her very first assemblage came about following a tumultuous incident involving her first husband, Robin Bartlett.

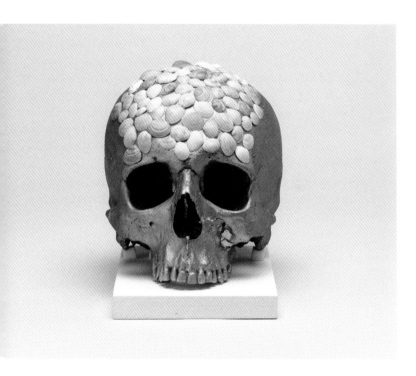

8. *Untitled Assemblage*, 1921–4, human skull painted
gold and decorated with small seashells

After their separation, Agar returned to their shared studio to collect her things and discovered a human skull, acquired by Bartlett during an anatomy lesson at the Slade. She retrieved the skull and returned it to Bartlett but his mother opened the parcel and, assuming it to be a cruel joke, furiously sent it back to Agar. Some years later she came across it again, painted it gold and decorated it with seashells (Fig. 8). The skull thus became her first assemblage, and inspired her to continue collecting a range of unusual and organic bits and pieces: 'I surround myself with fantastic bric-brac in order to trigger my imagination. For it is a certain kind of sensitive chaos that is creative, and not sterile order.'[26] Agar began to use the found object as a creative problem-solver, collecting stones, bones, horns, shells, figurines, textiles, ceramics, fossils, leaves and other oddments which she would use to provoke, spark or stir her imagination. *Untitled (Box)* (1935, Fig. 9) is a perfect example: an exquisite, vibrantly coloured box in which she laid an old dried seahorse on its back amongst flourishes of coral, shells and feathers, all wrapped in a fishing net.

Always on the lookout for flotsam and jetsam, Agar continued to beachcomb. In 1939, while staying in the French fishing-port Carquieranne, she saw: 'a fisherman cursing because he had brought up a Greek Amphora in his nets and it had torn his nets and nets are very expensive ... and I said to him "I'll have that".'[27] To it she added a ram's horn from Cumberland, a dried starfish and a couple of other sea-encrustations and: 'it was short work making *Marine Object*' (1939, Fig. 10).[28] *Marine Collage* (1939, Fig. 11) was made the same year and employs many of the same principles of chance, as well as a combination of sea creatures and classical imagery, this time in paper. Divided into four sections – like *The Autobiography of an Embryo* (see Fig. 7) but arranged in a portrait format – Agar leads the viewer through an accumulation of fish, snakes, leeches and lamprey, all carefully laid out within the silhouettes of four heads or busts. The silhouetted forms appear as

9. *Untitled (Box)*, 1935, mixed media box, paper, coral, feathers, Eye of Horus, cotton, watercolour, dried seahorse

10. *Marine Object*, 1939, terracotta, horn, bone and shells

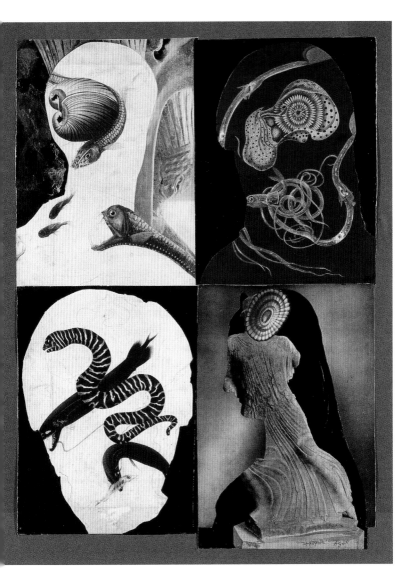

11. *Marine Collage*, 1939, collage on paper

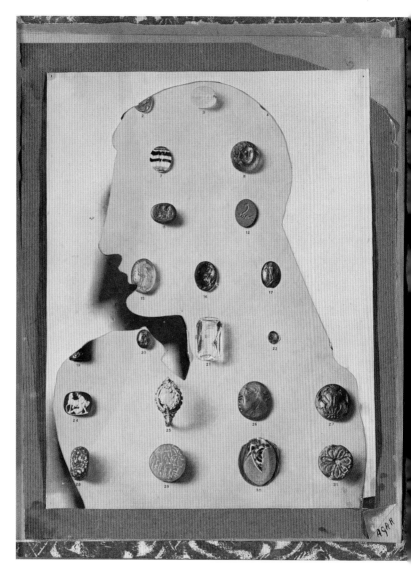

12. *Precious Stones*, 1936, collage on paper

'cut-outs' so that the various aquatic animals seem to swim through the minds of these figures – recalling that frequently drawn parallel between the subconscious and the depths of the ocean.

The silhouette of a head in profile would become a recurring motif for Agar, the earliest example can be found, again, in *The Autobiography of an Embryo*, where it appears a number of times. Then in *Precious Stones* (1936, Fig. 12), one of Agar's most significant collages, where a male face in profile becomes the central form. Pasted onto a white sheet of paper and framed by a third sheet, which forms a red border around the image, the silhouette is cut from a book on gemstones. The grid-like arrangement of numbered stones jars with the fluid outline of the portrait which – literally – cuts into the gems' categorical arrangement. A touching tribute to Bard, who was an avid collector of precious stones, the work also suggests an homage to certain historical styles of embossed portraiture on coins or stamps. And at a deeper level, it reflects Agar's tussle between order and tradition, and her interest in organic forms and the natural world.

The Surprise of Surrealism

Through her explorations in collage and assemblage, as well as her symbolic approach to abstraction, Agar was working within a conspicuously Surrealist vein, although she would never fully accept the moniker of Surrealist. She acknowledged the tradition of a kind of proto-Surrealism in Britain, which she saw in the works of William Blake, Lewis Carroll and Richard Dadd, and was content to come from a nation 'so predisposed to the expression of dream states and the unconscious mind.'[29] That said, it was with a feeling of gracious surprise that she invited Roland Penrose and Herbert Read into her studio in the spring of 1936. Penrose and Read were conducting studio visits in order to curate – with poet David Gascoyne – the

International Surrealist Exhibition. They selected three oil paintings and five objects from Agar's studio, much to her astonishment: 'the sudden attention took me by surprise. One day I was an artist exploring highly personal combinations of form and content, and the next I was calmly informed I was a Surrealist!'[30]

The most celebrated of Agar's works included in the exhibition was her large, four-section painting *Quadriga* (1935, Fig. 13) which consists of four carnivalesque horse heads, inspired by a photograph that Agar had taken of the Acropolis: 'I had long admired a photograph I had of a horse's head ... and I wondered in what strange way I could make it into a painting which could bridge the gap between the centuries ... I thought: this is a very lovely looking thing, and so I copied the outline of it, and inside I made all sorts of strange patterns and didn't have an eye or a mouth of a horse, or ears. I just made an absolute silhouette and then I put what I wanted inside.'[31] In Agar's treatment, the four heads are ghost-like, frantic and rhythmic – expressing movement and anxiety, each square different, building a mood. As with *The Autobiography of an Embryo* (see Fig. 7) and *Marine Collage* (see Fig. 11), Agar gives us a narrative, storyboarded across multiple panels and developing through order and disorder, rationality and irrationality. Hidden forms emerge, fluid outlines of mountains and seascapes recall mythological references to Pegasus or Selene, or even to the Four Horses of the Apocalypse: 'war was encroaching on the selfish peace of England: the Spanish Civil War acted as a kind of distant prelude to the Second World War, and it was to be many years before the Four Horsemen allowed their steeds to return to my frame.'[32]

Surrealism was certainly founded as a Pacifist reaction to the threat of Fascism in Europe, which Agar described as being 'shamefully ignored in England.'[33] In Read's introduction to the International Surrealism Exhibition, he described the artists

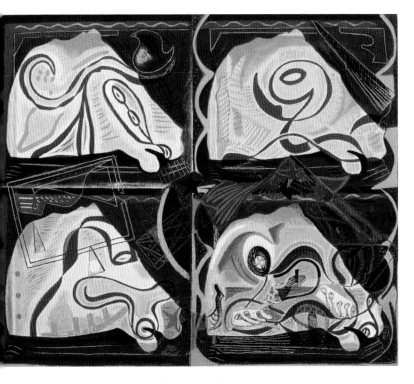

13. *Quadriga*, 1935, oil on canvas

14. *Angel of Anarchy*, 1936–40, plaster, fabric, shells,
beads, diamante stones and other materials

inside as too 'profoundly convinced of the rottenness of our civilisation to want to save a shred of its respectability.'[34] The exhibition was a controversial success: the galleries were crowded with visitors and public opinion was split between celebratory acclaim and condemnation of the grounds of depravity. But as Agar comments: 'the Surrealist's aim was not to establish a glorious place for themselves in the annals of art and literature, but to change the world. To transform life itself.'[35] Fascism was on the rise and the threat to free expression loomed ever greater. The following year, Agar exhibited with the Surrealists again in *Surrealist Objects and Poems* at the London Gallery (1937). Once again, Read's opening address was political: 'approach, for we have names to sell – angels of anarchy and machines for making clouds.'[36] Within this increasingly agitated climate, Agar exhibited *Angel of Anarchy* (1936–40, Fig. 14). The sculpture began as an ordinary plaster head modelled on Bard. However, when she received the first version of the plaster head back from the workshop Agar was initially dismayed by the 'deadness' of the white plaster – 'it looked like a death sculpture',[37] so she adorned it with pieces of white doyley, paper, black fur, embroidered silk, gem stones, seashells and ostrich feathers. While some of the elements suggest facial features, others are decorative accessories or jewellery. Feathers appear as wayward tufts of hair as well as features of an elaborate headdress. Similarly, the patterned textile is both a skin and a blindfold, creating ambiguous allusions to seduction and submissiveness, as well as a block or blinkering of Europe's uncertain political future.[38]

A second sculpture, *Angel of Mercy* (Fig. 15) was also modelled on Bard and forms the companion work to *Angel of Anarchy*. Dated 1934, it is now accepted that Agar likely worked on both at the same time, completing *Angel of Mercy* around 1939. In effect, Agar was turning on its head the Surrealist tendency of making a beautiful woman into a muse, taking Bard for hers – both her good angel and her bad one – mercy and anarchy.

Mercy is less a fetish figure and more benign than *Anarchy*, reminiscent of Agar's earlier decorative lines (akin to *Movement in Space*, see Fig. 4, and *Family Trio*, see Fig. 6) with gentler hues and soft, humorous additions: a dice in the nose, the star of the chin and the veil of eyelashes that cover his eyes.

Agar was certainly astute to the duplicitous gender expectations among the Surrealists: 'double-standards seem to have proliferated, and the women came off worse ... The men were expected to be very free sexually, but when a woman adopted the same attitude the hypocritical upset was tremendous.'[39] Aware of the fact that they were often reduced to the role of muse, the women of Surrealism reappropriated their appearances toward their shared artistic interests, dressing glamorously because: 'our concern with appearance was not a result of pandering to masculine demands, but rather a shared attitude to life and style ... The juxtaposition by us of a Schiaparelli dress with outrageous behaviour or conversation was simply carrying the beliefs of Surrealism into public existence.'[40] *Ladybird* (1936, Fig. 16) is a strong example of Agar's reappropriation of her own image, as well as perpetuating her passion for layering, collage and symbolism. The work consists of a black-and-white photograph of her taken by Bard in which she holds a sheet of transparent material in front of her naked body. Agar then drew on top of the image with sinuous lines, hands, discs, stars – and a ladybird – to create a sensual and empowering depiction of herself as an artist in her own right.

After the International Surrealism Exhibition ended in July 1936, to escape the hullabaloo, Agar and Bard travelled to Brittany, landing in Ploumanach after choosing to disembark there when, from the train window, Agar saw 'the fantastic rocks ... like enormous prehistoric monsters sleeping on the turf above the sea: a great buttock ending in a huge thumb, or a gigantic head tuned with organ pipes, a crowd, or a foot rearing up like a dolmen, all sculpted by the sea, that master-worker of time.'[41] The following day she travelled to the nearest town

15. *Angel of Mercy*, 1934, plaster with collage and watercolour

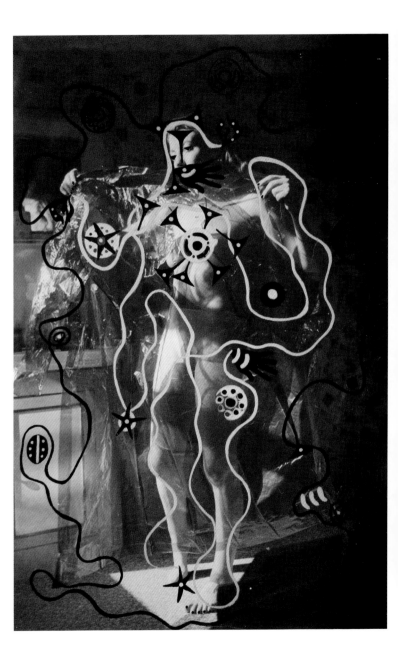

and purchased a Rolleiflex camera that would become her trusted companion for years to come. The photographs Agar took in Brittany of the Ploumanach rocks were to become an enduring source of inspiration – first as photographic works in their own right (Figs 17, 18) and then, in later years, as the basis for many a drawing and painting (see Fig. 26). Agar saw the rocks as naturally occurring works of art and cherished their Surrealist tendencies, which, as ever, she sought to combine with more rational abstraction. 'Surrealism for me draws inspiration from nature … Abstraction would also be exerting its influence upon me, giving me the benefit of geometry and design to match and balance and strengthen the imaginative elements of a composition. Outer eye and inner eye, backward and forward, inside out and upside down.'[42]

A Physical and Spiritual Famine: The Second World War and its Aftermath

By 1939, Agar had appeared in Surrealist exhibitions all over the world and was exhibiting regularly in London. However, as with many artists of her generation, the onset of war was to interrupt her artistic activity significantly. Nonetheless, the political climate did prompt Agar to propose marriage to Bard: 'the prospect of instant annihilation tends to put a new complexion on all relationships … We chose Leap Year Day of 1940 for our wedding, as this way we would have fewer anniversaries … !'[43] After their wedding, Agar and Bard both enlisted in the war effort, Agar volunteering in a canteen on Savile Row that served hot meals to civil servants. The role meant that she was able to stay in London and thus she kept her studio, though she felt little able to work: 'I felt it impossible to concentrate on painting when you could turn to look out of the window and see … a Messerschmidt [sic] flying low over

16. *Ladybird*, 1936, photograph with gouache and ink on paper

17. *Le Lapin, Ploumanach Rocks*, 1936, photograph

18. *Rock Form*, 1936–7, frottage and crayon on paper

the tree tops.'[44] Agar and Bard also served as Fire Watchers on night duty, taking it in turns to sit up through the night. Their London home became host to many friends and colleagues, either travelling through London to safety or newly homeless due to the Blitz.

Despite building apprehension, Agar continued to exhibit during the war and found collage – with its more political foundations and direct symbolism – a medium she could maintain: 'how does one communicate with any subtlety when the world is being deafened by explosions?'[45] In 1942 she had a solo exhibition at Redfern Gallery where she showed 24 new collages. One of these, *Erotic Landscape* (1942, Fig. 19) depicts a cut-out photograph of a nude woman, surrounded by a fanfare of plant and marine life, wave-like drawings and twisting, cellular tendrils. A girthy tree trunk grows sideways in the top left corner and a small spikey, black triangle peeps out of the woman's crotch. The work is dense and loaded, here desire feels violent and urgent, as though Agar is trying to summon all that is sensual and natural to surmount the struggles of war.

As the war ended, Agar 'felt like something new and marvellous ought to happen, but I was exhausted and humdrum, more tired and dispirited than usual.'[46] She describes this period as a physical and spiritual famine, trapped in London and emotionally drained by the anxieties of the last five years. Yearning for a change of scene but with travel outside of the country banned, she and Bard visited Cornwall and Ireland to replenish their imaginations. Slowly Agar returned to painting as if she were 'renewing a belief in life itself.'[47] Possibly the first painting she made after the end of the war, *Dance of Peace* (1945, Fig. 20) embodies this budding and tentative optimism. Painted in pastel washes and bucolic forms, the arrangement of dancing figures seems to draw directly from Agar's processes of collage, layering and overlapping as semi-translucent animals, leaves and faces emerge between the main figures. In direct contrast to the violence of war and the rapid social changes it had wrought, *Dance of Peace* recalls a pastoral idyll, looking back to humankind's rural past.

In 1948 Agar was invited to appear on *Eye of the Artist* – a television programme about the endeavours of Surrealism. She was asked to create an assemblage live on air, which she titled *Phantom of the Sea* (now lost). Agar was a huge success and was asked to take part on another programme devoted to hats, which had always been a point of fascination for Agar, most likely due to her mother's enduring passion for them: 'and what hats! Enormous constructions of straw, velvet or fur-like frigates under sail or birds on the wing. Embellished with vast bows, ribbons or ostrich feathers. I have a particular fondness for making hat-shaped surrealistic objects and have sometimes thought that, for instance, my *Ceremonial Hat for Eating Bouillabaisse* . . . might have been inspired by my mother's spectacular headgear.'[48] Indeed, on this second television appearance, Agar presented her yet-to-be-seen-by-the-public *Ceremonial Hat for Eating Bouillabaisse* (1936, Figs 1 and 21), wearing the remarkable construction on camera. Formed from a circular cork basket painted blue, topped with various found objects such as a fishnet, a lobster's tail, a starfish, and pieces of bones and coral, Agar described the hat as 'a sort of Arcimboldo headgear for the fashion conscious.'[49]

Over the next ten years, 'still aware of a sense of despondency . . . and threatened by morbidity',[50] Agar and Bard travelled to Sweden, Italy and Tenerife, embracing their re-established freedom. Agar was gradually working herself out the gloom of the war and Tenerife – where they returned for many summers – was to become 'a watershed in my life. For I had been suffering from a painter's dreaded middle period. I had been too long cut off from the world of nature, too cooped up . . . too cribbed and confined . . . and the relief of finding one's roots responding to the quickening pulse of vegetation, the vast mountain-scapes,

19. (overleaf) *Erotic Landscape*, 1942, collage on paper

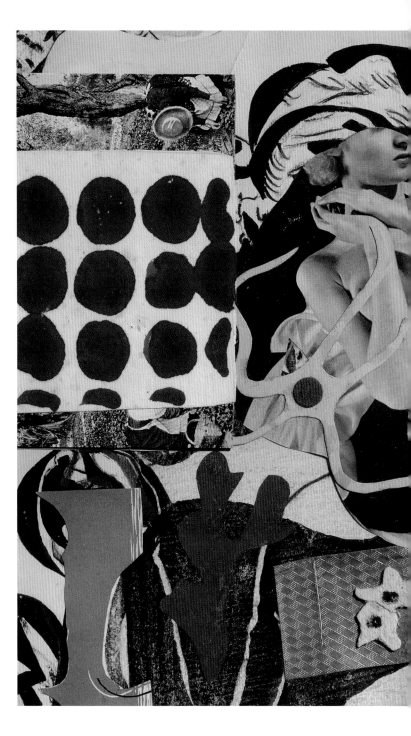

20. *Dance of Peace*, 1945, collage and gouache on paper

21. *Ceremonial Hat for Eating Bouillabaisse*, 1936, cork, coral,
sea-shells, fishbone and sea-urchin

22. *Frottage, Tenerife*, 1953, crayon on paper

the sea horizons … giving one a marvellous sense of liberation … all this made me fall in love with that mountainous dew-drop in the ocean and I revived and could work again.'[51] *Frottage, Tenerife* (1953, Fig. 22) demonstrates her revitalisation. Agar did not often use the Surrealist technique of frottage (a means of capturing the trace of a place or object by placing a piece of paper over an uneven surface then rubbing the paper with a drawing tool), but here she employs it skilfully, dreamily rendering the contrast between the sub-tropical vegetation of the island and its more arid, volcanic deserts.

Making Room for Joy: Late Painting and the Discovery of Acrylic

In 1958 Agar and Bard moved into a house – with a larger studio – in Kensington. She was enjoying a successful period of painting, travelling and exhibiting and had begun to feel like herself again, able to cultivate her own happiness: 'surely room must be made for joy in this world? There has to be hope and celebration.'[52] Her work was beginning to blur the divisions between collage, drawing and painting and she continued to experiment with Surrealist techniques such as automatism, frottage and decalcomania.[53]

One of Agar's most striking uses of automatism can be found in the small portrait of her friend, the poet Dylan Thomas, painted seven years after he had died and 30 years after she had first made a sketch of him at a party. She recalls: 'a ruddy faced cherub with a snub nose and no chin … squatted on the floor and began reciting limericks – a deep flow of bawdy nonsense that kept everyone enthralled … I managed to grab a pencil and paper and did some lightening drawings of this ugly suckling.'[54] *Head of Dylan Thomas* (1960–2, Fig. 23) uses the portrait-in-profile style already employed in several earlier works, though here Agar's experiments with automatism, or spontaneous painting, mean that Thomas' face is much more

23. *Head of Dylan Thomas*, 1960–2, oil paint and acrylic paint on board

loosely outlined in fluid white strokes and drips, atop a canvas that is full of red, purple and black abstract motifs. The flowing compositional style of this work is conceivably a deliberate homage to the free spirit of Thomas himself, the end result being the creation of a jubilant feeling or aura emanating from the chaotic and darkened background.

Throughout the 1960s Agar continued to exhibit and held her first retrospective at Brook Street Gallery in 1964 as well as participating in the London Group Jubilee exhibition the same year. More significant perhaps was her discovery in 1965 of acrylic paint, which was a revelation for Agar: it was easy to handle, quick drying and 'very versatile, it can be used as impasto, with a palette knife, or a thin wash gives wonderful glazes ... in acrylic I had found what I considered to be an ideal medium, and I wanted to both master and stretch it.'[55] This new development was wonderfully showcased at Agar's retrospective at the Commonwealth Institute in 1971, at which she showed 76 works and which Roland Penrose heralded as 'masterly'.[56] One of the works, *Slow Movement* (1970, Fig. 24) hints at the deep, persevering magic that Agar had been pursuing for the majority of her creative life. Inspired by the Ludovisi Throne, a Roman marble panel which shows Aphrodite bring raised from the sea by two handmaidens, Agar was keen to explore the upward movement of the women's arms. Although her painting is markedly different in style from the classical image, she retains the gentle sweep of their action, their elegant touch and languid sense of entwined movement. Her pale blue palette is dreamlike in tone while also reminiscent of one of the painting's main sources of inspiration (and enduring influence for Agar) – the sea.

In 1975, after several years of ill-health, Joseph Bard passed away: 'the silk thread of his life had spun itself out.'[57] Grief-stricken, Agar didn't paint for several years, instead writing Bard's biography. Over time, her notes on their life together also formed the basis of her autobiography, and she found the

24. *Slow Movement*, 1970, oil on canvas

process to be hugely restorative. In 1979 she embarked on painting *Bride of the Sea* (Fig. 25), a celebration of her time spent at the seashore – with Bard – and the location for many a found-object-treasure-hunt. Here again we see the silhouetted portrait-in-profile, this time amidst an amorphous mass of green, blue and brown forms: a ship's hull and mast, fishing nets, fish, anemones and several harlequinesque patterns. This late work, created when Agar was 80, could be a rumination on the formal and emotional connections between humans and the natural world, a lasting theme for Agar. Its strong autobiographical emphasis might also be interpreted as reflections on her creative life; the profiled face emerging from and sinking back into the content, colours and shapes of the sea.

In 1984, Agar returned to the photographs she had taken at Ploumanach almost 50 years before (see Figs 17, 18). In an exhibition at New Art Centre the same year, she presented an intrepid series of hallucinatory drawings and paintings inspired by these images: 'images so strong that they had imprinted themselves on my unconscious to be awakened decades later from their slumbers and appear in paint, resurrected by the womb of time and the oceans of the moon onto the grassy plains of Ploumanach.'[58] In these works she makes striking colour choices, jarring blues against browns, oranges and greens: her compositions are bold in their departure from the source imagery as she shifts perspectives, causing the rocks to loom over their landscape like anthropomorphised monsters. *Ploumanach Rocks* (1984, Fig. 26) thus represents a remarkable late expression of Agar's inimitable aesthetic sensibility – a series of works which look back to past lives as well as giving a self-conscious reflection on the force of imagination.

Agar's autobiography, *A Look at My Life* was published in 1988 and in 1990 she was elected to the Royal Academy, a fact that amused her greatly: 'I'd always rather laughed at the

25. (overleaf) *Bride of the Sea*, 1979, acrylic on canvas

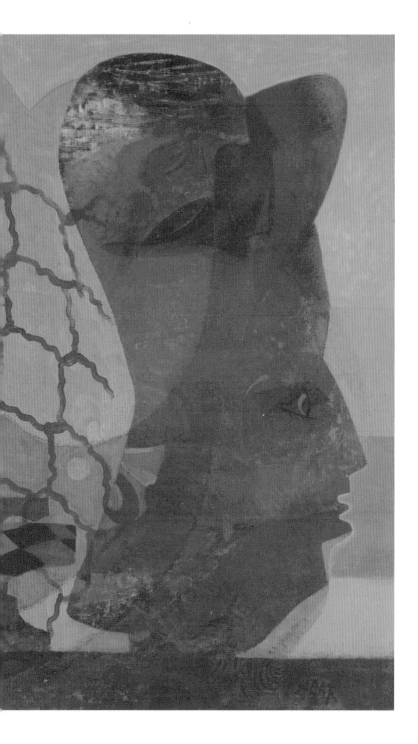

26. (above and opposite) *Ploumanach Rocks*, 1984, acrylic on canvas

Royal Academy . . . but evidently now they take every sort! They wouldn't have surrealists at one time you see, they wanted to be completely academic.'[59]

Throughout her long career as an artist, Agar rarely stood still, she was continually experimenting and exploring, utilising a wide range of techniques, media, symbols and subject matter, all along the parallel paths of abstraction and Surrealism: 'the two movements that interested me most . . . I see nothing incompatible in that, indeed we walk on two legs, and for me, one is abstract, the other surreal – it is point and counterpoint.'[60]

Notes

1   Eileen Agar, *A Look at My Life* (London 1988), p.232
2   The London Group is a society based in London, England, originally created to offer additional exhibiting opportunities to artists besides the Royal Academy of Arts. It was established in 1913 by 32 artists including Walter Sickert, Ethel Sands, Nan Hudson, Jacob Epstein, Wyndham Lewis, David Bomberg and Henri Gaudier Brzeska.
3   Ibid., p.121
4   Ibid., p.25
5   Ibid., p.34
6   Ibid., p.42
7   Ibid., p.48
8   Ibid., p.65
9   Ibid., p.52
10 Ibid., p.73
11 British Library National Life Stories: Artists' Lives: Eileen Agar interviewed by Cathy Courtney, Apr–Aug 1990, https://sounds.bl.uk/related-content/TRANSCRIPTS/021T-C0466X0001XX-ZZZZA0.pdf, p.34 (date accessed 9/1/2020)
12 *A Look at My Life*, p.73
13 Ibid., p.85
14 Ibid., p.93
15 Ibid., p.93
16 Much of this furniture is now in the collection of the Victoria and Albert Museum, London.
17 *A Look at My Life*, p.101
18 Ibid., p.97
19 Eileen Agar, quoted in Ann Simpson, David Gascoyne and Andrew Lambirth, *Eileen Agar 1899–1991* (Edinburgh 1999), p.19
20 British Library National Life Stories: Artists' Lives (see note 11), p.83
21 Eileen Agar quoted in *Illustrated Catalogue of Acquisitions 1986–88* (London 1996), p.240
22 Ibid.
23 *A Look at My Life*, p.147

24 Ibid., p.111

25 Now held within the Tate Collection.

26 Ibid., p.148

27 British Library National Life Stories: Artists' Lives (see note 11), p.62

28 *A Look at My Life*, p.144

29 Ibid., p.114

30 Ibid., p.115

31 British Library National Life Stories: Artists' Lives (see note 11), p.60

32 *A Look at My Life*, p.122

33 Ibid., p.123

34 Ibid.

35 Ibid., p.148

36 Ibid., p.123

37 British Library National Life Stories: Artists' Lives (see note 11), p.67

38 It seems that anarchy was indeed in the air in 1937 and the sculpture was anarchic enough to go missing after an exhibition in Amsterdam in 1938, never to be seen again, though evidence of it does exist on the cover of the *Surrealist Objects and Poems* catalogue from 1937. Agar therefore made another version – which we have now come to know as *Angel of Anarchy* – which is more radical, theatrical and anarchic in its adornments.

39 *A Look at My Life*, p.121

40 Ibid. 120

41 Ibid., p.124

42 Ibid., p.121

43 Ibid., p.150

44 Ibid., p.153

45 Ibid., p.157

46 Ibid., p.161

47 Ibid., p.165

48 Ibid., p.19

49 Ibid., p.168

50 Ibid., p.177

51 Ibid., p.186

52 Ibid., p.197

53 Decalcomania is a technique developed by the Surrealists (primarily Ithell Colquhoun, Max Ernst and Oscar Dominguez) in which paint is pressed between two surfaces. The most common example of decalcomania involves applying paint to paper then folding it, applying pressure and then unfolding the paper to reveal a mirror pattern.

54 Ibid., p.108

55 Ibid., p.202

56 Of the exhibition, Penrose wrote: 'I find that I am led into deep sensations of time and space in some recent paintings where sharply delineated

forms hover in darkness so that the blackness that surrounds them and is alive in its own right, and others where transparent forms with softer edges merge together creating new volumes and a magic sense of depth, a vortex of colour which carries the eye with rhythmic motion into a realm which transcends our limited field of observation. Quoted in *Eileen Agar 1899–1991*, p.33

57 *A Look at My Life*, p.213
58 Ibid., p.1
59 Ibid., p.229
60 Ibid.

Image credits

1. *Ceremonial Hat for Eating Bouillabaisse*, 1936, black and white photograph, private collection. Photograph courtesy Bridgeman Images.
2. *Self-portrait*, 1927, oil on canvas, 765 × 641 mm, National Portrait Gallery, London.
3. *Three Symbols (Flying Pillar)*, 1928–30, oil on canvas, 1003 × 559 mm, Tate, London. Photograph © Tate.
4. *Movement in Space*, 1931, oil on canvas, 736 × 914 mm, J. Sheekey Restaurant, j-sheekey.co.uk @jsheekeyldn. Photograph courtesy Reaktion Books.
5. *The Bird. Two Lovers*, 1931, woodcut, 120 × 180 mm, The Court Gallery, Somerset. Photograph courtesy Reaktion Books.
6. *Family Trio*, 1931, watercolour, 310 × 330 mm, courtesy James Birch. Photograph courtesy Pallant House Gallery, Chichester © Andy Keate.
7. *The Autobiography of an Embryo*, 1933–4, oil on board, 914 × 2130 mm, Tate, London. Photograph © Tate.
8. *Untitled Assemblage*, 1921–4, human skull painted gold and decorated with small seashells, 157 × 122 × 150 mm, Tate, London. Photograph © Tate.
9. *Untitled (Box)*, 1935, mixed media box, paper, coral, feathers, eye of Horus, cotton and watercolour, 164 × 224 × 55 mm, The Murray Family Collection, UK and USA. Photograph courtesy Pallant House Gallery, Chichester © Richard Valencia.
10. *Marine Object*, 1939, terracotta, horn, bone and shells, 420 × 340 × 230 mm, Tate, London. Photograph © Tate.
11. *Marine Collage*, 1939, collage on paper, 580 × 410 mm, The Vera and Arturo Schwarz Collection of Dada and Surrealist Art in the Israel Museum. Photograph © The Israel Museum by Avshalom Avital.
12. *Precious Stones*, 1936, collage on paper, 260 × 209 mm, Leeds Museums and Galleries (Leeds Art Gallery). Photograph courtesy Bridgeman Images.
13. *Quadriga*, 1935, oil on canvas, 521 × 610 mm, courtesy The Penrose Estate.
14. (and Cover) *Angel of Anarchy*, 1936–40, plaster, fabric, shells, beads, diamante stones and other materials, 570 × 460 × 317 mm, Tate, London. Photograph © Tate.

15. *Angel of Mercy*, 1934, plaster with collage and watercolour, 445 mm (h), The Sherwin Collection, Leeds, UK. Photograph courtesy Bridgeman Images.
16. *Ladybird*, 1936, photograph with gouache and ink on paper, 760 × 508 mm, The Murray Family Collection, UK and USA. Photograph courtesy Reaktion Books.
17. *Photograph of 'Le Lapin' rock in Ploumanach, Brittany, France*, 1936, photograph, 63 × 60 mm, Tate, London. Photograph © Tate.
18. *Rock Form,* 1936–7, frottage and crayon on paper, 180 × 130 mm, private collection. Photograph courtesy Christies.
19. *Erotic Landscape*, 1942, collage on paper, 255 × 305 mm, private collection. Photograph courtesy Pallant House Gallery, Chichester © Doug Atfield.
20. *Dance of Peace*, 1945, collage and gouache on paper, collection of Kathryn Ludlow. Photograph courtesy Offer Waterman.
21. *Ceremonial Hat for Eating Bouillabaisse*, 1936, cork, coral, sea-shells, fishbone and sea-urchin, Victoria and Albert Museum, London.
22. *Frottage, Tenerife*, 1953, crayon on paper, 350 × 250 mm, The Redfern Gallery, London.
23. *Head of Dylan Thomas*, 1960–2, oil paint and acrylic paint on board, 600 × 435 mm, Tate, London. Photograph © Tate.
24. *Slow Movement*, 1970, oil on canvas, 1512 × 1512 mm, National Galleries of Scotland.
25. *Bride of the Sea*, 1979, acrylic on canvas, 760 × 1015 mm, Government Art Collection, UK. Photograph © Crown Copyright: UK Government Art Collection.
26. *Ploumanach Rocks*, 1984, acrylic on canvas, 600 × 600 mm. The Redfern Gallery, London.

About the author

Laura Smith was appointed Curator of Whitechapel Gallery in February 2018, where, among other exhibitions, she has worked on the first UK survey show of artist duo Elmgreen & Dragset (2018), a touring retrospective of Italian, Brazil-based artist Anna Maria Maiolino (2019), and with Helen Cammock, winner of the 2017–19 Max Mara Art Prize for Women. She is excited to be working with the next Max Mara winner, Emma Talbot on her forthcoming exhibition. Prior to joining the Whitechapel Gallery, Laura was Curator at Tate from 2012–18, where she was responsible for a series of international historic and contemporary projects by artists including Claude Cahun, Liliane Lijn, Linder, France-Lise McGurn, Marlow Moss, Nashashibi/Skaer, Lucy Stein, Jessica Warboys and Rebecca Warren, as well as group exhibitions such as *Virginia Woolf: An Exhibition Inspired by her Writings* (2018), *Turner Prize* (2016) and *Images Moving Out Onto Space* (2015).

Laura writes extensively on modern and contemporary art. Most recently she has contributed a chapter to Oxford University Press' *Virginia Woolf Reader* on Woolf's influence on the visual arts, and also an essay on Lisa Brice for her forthcoming monograph. She is a regular contributor to *frieze* magazine and *Art Review*.

Acknowledgements

This book wouldn't have been possible without the generosity and kindness of a number of institutions and individuals. I am grateful to all those who have provided images and given permissions for works in their collections to be reproduced – thank you, it is wonderful to see so many works by Agar illustrated here. I would also like to thank the Agar scholars who have made such valuable contributions to studies of her work; their research has made this book possible and I am particularly indebted to Andrew Lambirth, Michel Remy and Andrew Murray. The Estate of Eileen Agar and Redfern Gallery have been endlessly encouraging, helpful and supportive and I am ever appreciative of their assistance. Thank you too to Harriet Olsen, founder of Eiderdown Books, both for offering me this remarkable opportunity and for inspiring so many women with her all-woman publishing house.

I want to thank Enrico for everything. And – importantly – all the amazing women in my life: Willa, Julie, Jessica, Eleanor, Sophia, Violet, Doreen, Barbara, Christine, Sammi, Chloe, Emily, Quinn, Rebecca, Vivien, Rachel, Maria, Morgan, Lotta, Phoebe, Bryony, Sara, Rosza, Helen, Kay, Lucy, France-Lise, Naomi, Katie, Lily, Mette, Elizabeth, Clarrie, Penny, Emily, Yma, Pia, Regina and Vanessa.

Finally, I'd like to dedicate this book to Eileen Agar, whose never-ending curiosity, tenacity, self-belief and unbounded creativity should be an inspiration to us all.

Index

Eileen Agar
By Laura Smith
First Edition

First published in the United Kingdom in 2021 by Eiderdown Books
eiderdownbooks.com

Series conceived and developed by Eiderdown Books
Text © Laura Smith
Images © The Estate of Eileen Agar

The moral right of the author has been asserted.

A CIP record for this book is available from the British Library.

ISBN: 978-1-9160416-5-3

Edited by Rebeka Cohen
Indexed by Jan Worrall
Series design by Clare Skeats
Typeset by Clare Skeats in Lelo by Katharina Köhler

The Modern Women Artists logotype is set in Hesse Antiqua, which
was released in 2018 to mark the 100th birthday of Gundrun Zapf von
Hesse. The forms of Hesse Antiqua are based on the metal punches
that von Hesse created in 1947 while working as a bookbinder at the
Bauer Type Foundry in Frankfurt.

Printed and bound by Latitude

Reprographics by ALTA